A Sea of

LILACS

A Sea of
LILACS

Sorrow in Verse and Vignette

sarah elizabeth moore

For loved ones and caregivers who serve –
unpaid, untrained and unseen –
despite your own sorrow.

Your grief is my own.
And this book is for you.

All proceeds from the sale of this project will be donated to
a non-profit organization in honor of Momma Heidi.

Contents

TO THE READER

The earliest readers of this manuscript have expressed two incredible misunderstandings for which I am to blame. I offer this note both as a *mea culpa* and as an attempt to clarify these two crucial elements of the book you're about to read.

First is the idea that Momma Heidi was an amazing woman whom you should admire. She was, and you should, but these are quite secondary to this tome's purpose. It is not intended as a gift to my incredible mother. It is not my attempt to immortalize her (Jesus has already done this). It's not about honoring her. If you want to read words I've penned in honor of my mother, I have a slew of pieces on my public blog I can recommend. Just reach out to me. While I hope this collection does paint a lovely portrait of the woman I so adored in this life, it's simply not about her.

This book is a gift to the loved ones of those suffering a slow, difficult death. These brave and broken souls serve as caregivers, not out of conviction or commitment, but often simply out of a love too stubborn to forfeit any moment they still have with their loved one. Though the devastation fractures their hearts over and again, they hear the slowing of the clock and cling desperately to each tick that remains. This paradox of heartache and hope is more real than words.

In my own experience, I ached for someone to understand, not merely with words of compassion, but with the true soul recognition of someone who had been through it and lived to tell. Because honestly, there were many, many moments I didn't think I would survive caregiving.

And that brings me to the second *mea culpa*, which is perhaps more complicated.

I cannot ease the weight of this book.

If I could ease the weight of this book, I would refuse, because the moments that birthed these poems and vignettes were real. They were heavy. They were suffocating. They were not logical. There was neither order nor sense to be made of them. They were simply hard. Or maybe – they were complicatedly hard. But they were also good. There were moments of beauty and hope in the storm of my mother's dying. I clung to those moments and memories with every last ounce of strength. I cling to them still. You'll catch a few of them as you read this book, and I pray you'll recognize such moments in your own journey. There is beauty and hope to be found, despite the heartache.

That being said, if the poems are too heavy for where you're at – skip to the vignettes. They're a bit light-hearted-er. They're more focused on those good moments I still cherish of my mother.

I hope that what I'm about to say here doesn't cause you to set this book down; I'd really like you to read it. But the truth is this: Those who have acted as caregivers (whether for an evening, a week, or a lifetime) know and recognize that the heaviest, most difficult moments cannot possibly make it to paper. They know, I think, that this book represents only a fraction of the moments that broke me.

And some of those moments were written from a different perspective - even my mother's - to honor the very real heartache of moments experienced by others. I explore these different points of view in the title poem, *Sea of*

Lilacs, as well as several of the vignettes. These were experiences I witnessed from folks who were affected by Momma Heidi's life and death in a very meaningful way.

The reader will find, I hope, comfort in knowing that other souls have been in that place of heartache as they try to live with the very blatant reality of death that consumes all their senses.

If that is you, I wrote this book for you. I welcome you into these pages, hoping you find solace and validation and courage to press on.

If that is not you, I welcome you into these pages just the same, because someday it could be you; someday it could be someone you love.

With all my heart,

PROLOGUE
The Diagnosis.

I heard the rattle of her car as it pulled down our dirt road, then the silence as she parked and turned off the engine.

"She's here, Momma. Are you ready?"

"I think so," Mom said.

I stood to open the door when I heard her footsteps on the porch.

"Hi!" She greeted me with a hug, as if we weren't meeting for the first time. "You must be Sarah. I'm Nurse Carla."

I choked back my tears, and she held me there for a moment. She whispered, "It's alright. That's why I start with a hug."

"Come in, please."

Mom was struggling to stand from her recliner. Carla went right to her, put her arm around Mom's shoulders, and helped her up.

"Well, Nurse Heidi! You look just the same as the last time I saw you! Can I hug you?"

"Of course!" Mom's face beamed like the morning sun. I swallowed my emotions again as this stranger embraced my mother.

"It's okay if you don't remember me," the nurse said. "But when I started working at the hospital, you were my orientation nurse on the Birthing Unit. You taught me everything I know about how to birth a baby! And then when I had my son, you were my delivery nurse, so you taught me everything else I know about how to birth a baby!"

"Oh! You have a little boy!" Mom exclaimed, and Carla helped her sit back down in her recliner. "I'm sorry, I don't remember."

"Oh, heavens, don't be sorry. You delivered so many babies in your career. And it was a long time ago." Carla sat on the sofa where she'd be nearest Mom. "He just turned twenty-two and graduated from college. I think the last time I saw you was when he was born. But you're just as beautiful now as you were then. I always loved your dark, curly hair."

"Not so dark anymore," Mom smiled. "And not so curly. It's a bit thin these days."

"Aren't we all?" Carla touched her hair. "Age happens to us all, Heidi!"

"I suppose that's true."

"Well, Heidi, from what your daughter has told me, it sounds like you haven't been feeling so well lately. Would it be okay if I asked you some questions? See if there's anything we can do to help you?"

"Yes, I would like that."

"Would you like me to step out?" I asked. I saw the panic flash in Mom's eyes.

"I think it might help if you stayed, as long as it's okay with Heidi."

"Please stay," Mom said. "I might need your help answering some things."

I sat in the rocking chair opposite Mom so she could see me.

Carla pulled a notepad and pen from her bag, crossed her legs, and said, "So Heidi, your family is concerned that you're not feeling well. How are you feeling today?"

Carla spent the next forty-five minutes asking about Mom's health and medical history.

We spoke about the sudden, debilitating hip pain Mom experienced just after Thanksgiving in 2017. How we'd been in and out of the Emergency Department with no diagnosis. How we'd struggled to get Mom to appointments with her General Practitioner, a Neurosurgeon, and a Physical Therapist – the last of whom refused to physical-therapy anything because he said it was clear there was something wrong and he wasn't willing to manipulate her joint without knowing what was actually going on in there. How we literally had to lift her up and down off of the toilet because her hip pain was excruciating. How it took two of us to get her to appointments because she simply couldn't put any weight on her leg.

We spoke about the night her face turned gray and my brother and I took her to the Emergency Department at the "other" hospital because we couldn't bear the thought of being sent home without a diagnosis again. How her kidneys had shut down from pain meds, NSAIDs, and dehydration. How she was transferred to the "big" hospital for admission and she spent Christmas recovering from what the hospitalist called "a perfect storm of kidney failure," where her kidneys just took too many blows from too many directions.

We spoke about her discharge from that stay, still without any diagnosis pertaining to her hip pain. How we continued struggling to keep Mom comfortable. How she couldn't sleep more than forty-five minutes at a time without being repositioned. How we tried to get her into the car to take her to her follow-up with her GP after the kidney failure, and we got stuck in the garage – on a cold January morning – because she could neither sit down on the car seat nor step back up the three steps to get into the house. How we had to call for an ambulance and then listened to the ER doctor tell us Mom simply had "a touch of bursitis."

We spoke about the "touch of bursitis" moment, and how my brother likely saved Mom's life by insisting that another physician come and evaluate Mom. How the "another physician" recognized Mom from his time rounding on the Birthing Unit, and how finally – after six weeks of this struggle – he was the first physician to physically examine her hip. How he had barely touched her and she cried out in pain, her body literally lurching off the ER bed. How he admitted her and ordered a sample drawn

14

from her hip joint the next morning, which would show what we'd been battling all along: A staph aureus infection.

We spoke about the long road of IV antibiotics, the surgery to remove the diseased bone and place a cement spacer infused with antibiotics, and eventually, the hip replacement itself. How all the while, Mom battled delusions and hallucinations. How her memory had essentially "stopped," and she'd lost more than a year of memory.

We spoke of the continued decline of Mom's memory. How some days she seemed fine, and others, it was as if we were right back into the delusions and hallucinations. How she had been evaluated by the neurologist who called it "dementia" but didn't really give us more than that, except pills that didn't bring much relief.

And we spoke, finally, of the past year. How Mom had lost much weight. How her memory was rapidly crumbling. And how she could no longer be alone in the house – how she refused even to sleep alone in her bedroom – because the hallucinations were so terrifying to her at times.

Nurse Carla reached for Mom's hand and squeezed it.

"You've been through so much, Heidi."

"I didn't know," Mom told her. "I don't remember any of it. How awful this must be for my children."

"From what I've heard, your children are so thankful you're still with them!"

I nodded. "We all love you, Momma. We just want to be sure we're getting you the help you need."

"And I think, Heidi, that we're in the right place. Hospice sounds like a good fit for where you're at. You said, Sarah, that the neurologist didn't give you a definitive diagnosis?"

"He just said it was dementia."

"Well," Carla looked me straight in the eye, "If Heidi were our patient, we would diagnose this as Lewy Body Disease. Everything about her medical ordeal the past several years – even the seemingly out-of-nowhere hip infection – points to Dementia with Lewy Bodies."

"Lewy Body?" I don't think I'd ever been more shocked in my life. "What? How? What?"

"In fact," she continued, "the neurologist wrote in his note that he believed it to be Lewy Body Disease. It's very common for the manifestation of Lewy Body to occur in conjunction with a seemingly unrelated medical crisis."

"Like a hip infection?"

"Like a hip infection. But the truth is, Lewy Body has been going on in your mom's system since before the hip infection. We find that people like your mother, who are intelligent and academically minded, tend to compensate for the symptoms of Lewy Body early on without even realizing it."

She spoke with us for some time about how Lewy Body is different from other dementias. and the more she shared, the more clearly I saw my mother in the details.

"Am I dying?" My mother asked.

"No, Heidi. You're not dying. But there is no cure for Lewy Body Disease. It will cause your body to die."

"How long?" Mom choked.

"Oh, honey, only the good Lord knows. But I'll be honest with you. Hospice care is for patients whose natural disease progression will likely lead to death within six months. Based on the changes your family has seen in this past year, we are there, Heidi. You are in the final stages of Lewy Body Disease, and I truly believe Hospice is the best care option for you and your family."

"Six months?" Something within me collapsed like an empire built of sand is swallowed up in one consuming wave of the sea. Innately, I'd known she was headed in this direction for some time. But the confirmation was perhaps too real to carry.

"We can bring help to you and your family right here in your home during your final months here and hopefully provide a bit of comfort and support to all of you. There's no cure for Lewy Body, but we do have tools and medications that can help quiet some of the sights and sounds that can make Lewy Body so scary."

"Six months." I whispered.

Carla nodded.

Five months later, we laid Mom to rest at the corner of Mallard and Eagle.

A Sea of Verse

A DOUBLE HAIKU FOR ALL SAINTS DAY

For Mommas Moore and Lamb

Grief – ever the proof
Of love's eternality –
Is indelible.

And joy – the first fruit
Of eternal fellowship –
Is worth every tear.

NOBODY TOLD ME

A Blessing for my Mother

Nobody told me
Death was so hard –
   That its coming could take a whole lifetime.

And nobody told me
How it would linger –
   Neither coming nor going – just stagnant, suspended,

Like the world outside
Before a storm –
   In silence, waits, neither longing nor dreading –

Just waiting.
Waiting.

Knowing
Rain is coming –
   It is upon us.

So we wait.
Silent.

It is holy, somehow.
This moment.

Even sparrows hush their song
Listening for that promised, threatened gift –
   As it taps to the ground with the first splash of life.

I don't know if they sing

Through the storm –
   Or if they hold their breath until it subsides.

But I know they wait silent,
Expecting, before –
   Ruffling feathers for warmth in the boughs of the
evergreens

Til the flickering skies unfurl in torrent –
A dance to the rhythm of Love and Thunder
The skies have turned
(And so I have turned)
To shards of glass,
Reflecting every glint of light.
Of lightning.

Yes, it is holy – Sacred – somehow.

And nobody said it would break me.
Nobody said it would shatter my core.

Yes, it is – Holy –
This torment, somehow –
This stepping from life into death
   To step from death into life.

And nobody told me it would be so hard
To watch you take these sacred steps
   To wait as you shift from one foot to the other
   To wear hope as my raiment while sorrows consume.

Nobody told me.

Nobody *told* me.

But you always told me –
There's something about a good storm that makes the peas
pop
   Pushing through the dirt to reach for the sun
 And this is the only thing I know right now.
 And it seems right.
It seems that you've been planted in Heaven's soil all
along.

So I pray it for your garden heart.

May the thunder of your Savior's Love
Call you to break through the surface of the soil;

May the heavens shower you,
Bathe you, cleanse you of all the cares of this world;

May you lean ever towards the light of His presence
Into life – true life – Everlasting.

Amen.

IT PASSES QUICKLY

Life –
it passes quickly
even when it's slow

One moment, split
Rended, broken
Between here and not.
Inhale – here.
Exhale – gone.
A jagged edge between life and death
that breaks its shards upon the hearts
of those left here to grieve
Etching deep like frozen steel
a wound that cannot heal
And somewhere, there, the memories of love –
they linger, still
like a perfume scent that never breaks
never dissipates.

Yes, life – it passes quickly.
Even when it's slow.

PRAYER HAIKU I

Jesus, calm my storm
Silence all the sorrow here
With your loving voice

PRAYER HAIKU II

Jesus, please be here
Drive the trauma far away
From my home and heart

PRAYER HAIKU III

Father, I need you
Redeem my ash and sackcloth
For your fragrant joy

EVEN BLUE INK

I'm weary – so weary – of bearing this load –
This life – and the Weight of my sorrows.
And I'm weary – so weary – of feeling alone
In this place where…
I can't even write a poem.
I can't find the words to convey where I've been or what
I'm feeling or …

I'm just so weary.
And sad.
So very sad.
How did I get here, completely estranged from my family?
From my friends?
From my guitar?
From my writing?

I miss my mom.
And I'm angry of it.
She's not even dead – she's just… gone.

And I'm sitting here, trying to make sense of
What doesn't make sense.
And it doesn't make sense why I can't make sense of it
With words or music or crafting or Scripture or
The ways I've traditionally made sense of life.
I know how to make sense of living.
With ink and cotton,
Cat gut and wool.

But dying is harder.
There's no sense to be making.
And even blue ink can't make it comply.

THERE'S A CRAVING

There is a wanting, a craving, a dying
For words
And rhythm and structure
And ink

Not for telling or showing, but my own understanding –
Making sense of the Chaos,
Making sense of Despair;
For silencing fear and failure and
the dozen dying houseplants –
a shallow breath
an echo in silence, reminding me –
Life is frail.
I am frail.

In all this mess – this tacit mess,
It's voice I've lost
or words, it seems.
So I'm struggling
To find normal
To find rhythm once again
In breath, in step, in heartbeat

BROKEN DOWN

Oh, my heart –
Broken down,
Weighted down,
Like cement
to Superior floor.

My dreams scattered –
Fluttered away,
Flung to the corners
Of the vast
Milky Way

I need gravity –
And ungravity –
Something to anchor
And buoy
My soul

GRIEF HAIKU I

I miss you more now
It's not getting easier
Sad resignation

GRIEF HAIKU II

If I let you go
I may forget the good parts
Still silenced by pain

GRIEF HAIKU III

I thought I was tired
Weary from love and caring
I was just grieving

GRIEF HAIKU IV

There were times so dark
So bitter in anguished soul
That I longed for death

To tell you the truth
I still long to disappear
Rather than recall

SPRING-WEATHERED TUNES

Neath a layer of ice on a deck full of Winter
And threats of the bitterest climes
A violet lingers in cold-crystalled soil
Waiting for tenderer times

When Day will restore frail tendrils of hope
And petals of withering hues
Now chilled by the song of bunkered-down birds
That sing only Spring-weathered tunes

UNSPEAKABLE

It is a grief unspeakable –
and so unspoken and – often – ignored,
tiptoed around and evaded

We cannot look it in the eye –
it terrifies the soul
it rips the heart out of the chest
we cannot look
we cannot speak
we cannot face the deep abyss
of losing one we love so dear

SLOW TO TURN

I just don't know if I can do this
Anymore –
The dying, the dying –
        Every moment – the dying
But never any nearer to
Death.

It suffocates –
        Strangles me –
Crushing my hyoid and
All the hopes I planted for Spring.

Come and bury me, Old Man Winter.
Let me rest awhile.
Summer leaves me weary
And Autumn leaves are
Slow
To
Turn.
Blow through Jack Pine's lanky trunk
To tousle Blue- and White-haired Spruce
Til all my friends fly far away
From cold
And snow
And laden bough

Except my faithful Chickadee
        Who serenades and lullabies me
(Perhaps she will dirge me, as well)
Every moment
Every day
Even as my breath fades –

The warmth of Life
Dispelled
By a death too slow to Come.

WINTER HAIKU I

A foot of fresh snow
Like a Second Burial:
Already cold stone

WINTER HAIKU II

Nothing is the same
All the world around me – changed
Now that you are gone

WINTER HAIKU III

Cannot sleep. Again.
I'm flooded with memories
Of November gales.

WINTER HAIKU IV

This year will make two
But it just feels like two days
Since we said goodbye

ARCHILOCHUS COLUBRIS

I've screwed up again.
It's too soon, they said.
The hummers won't be here for weeks.
It's still too cold.
Give it one more week.
The Migration Map.
Blah, blah, it's just too soon.

But I've seen the male Ruby thrice this week,
alighting on air, it seems,
where His feeders should be
and then turning toward the window to deadpan me.
  Where is Heidi?
  Where is my feeder?
  What have you done?

And I can't reply.
He leaves before I can open my mouth, so I
choke on words I just don't have for this mess I've made –
even for Him.
How do I tell Him she's gone?
How do I say the grief has shattered me through like the
subzero has shattered His feeders
because I failed to bring them in over winter?
How do I tell Him, now that He's here – *It's too soon?*
Everybody said it's too soon!
Will He southbound yet awhile if I pull out the Migration
Map?

Mom always said putting their feeders out after two or
three sightings was 'too little, too late.'
They'd look elsewhere for food after that.

44

But it's the only thing I know to do this morning.
Make the sugar water.
Clean the sole surviving feeder.
Fix its hanger.
Fill it full.
And sit by the window to wait.

And I'm ready now if He does return.
It's too soon, but I'm ready.
I'll just whisper the truth (it's all I have).
I'm sorry.

HALF A BREATH

It is in the space of half a breath –
not breathing in, but breathing out –
the exhale of fear, of hope, of life.

It is stilled.
It is silent.
Except for the grieving of those who love,
those who are left behind.

IT DOESN'T MATTER HOW

It doesn't matter how old you are –
seven or seventy –
losing your momma is a deep and
unspeakable
unquenchable
unsilenceable
Grief.

It is something deeper than sorrow
and more tangible than tears.
It is a bitter unraveling
of all that we know
of everything we hold dear.

But watching her die –
that is Torture
of the cruelest kind –
an agony unhealing,
unyielding,
enduring.

But you cannot bury the bitter recall
of seeing and hearing and smelling
her death
unless you bury the love, as well.

And do not do it – I pray you will not!
Remember each moment.
Remember it all.
Remember it well, Child –
Remember it well.

SPRING HAIKU I

Babies rooting out
From flowered, tendrilled spiders
Hope for tomorrow

SPRING HAIKU II

Three a.m. – sleepless
I'll crochet and think of you
And JV's fastball

CORAL TULIPS

Coral tulips,
reluctant to open –
    subtle in fragrance,
    fragile fierce petals cling to what is inside,
    like the graves of those gone but being reborn –
tilt ever-so-slightly toward the rays of dawn
sneaking through the eastern door this morn.

Reminders of spring
and redemption –
    and the knowing that Jesus is risen
    (He is risen indeed – Alleluia!)
    and I, too, shall rise with Him
    changed in an instant –
Incorruptible.

IT IS NOT THE DYING

It is not the dying, but the lingering of it
That wearies my heart now with grief
And it is not the sorrow or heartbreak I fear
But the feeling of utter relief

It's not the loathing that I know will find me
It's not all the words left unsaid
It's all of those things I never *could* say –
These are the things I'll regret

So many moments, carrying freely
The whisper of love on the wind
As it calls your name, bids you come
Leaving this world behind

It's not the saying goodbye I despise
But the saying it every day
As you slip nearer – and further – and nearer
And further, again – away

HALF A DOZEN PENS

I found a half a dozen pens
in Momma's old recipe box,
blue and black and black that's blue
and several, clearly, for trash
dried and dead –

oh except this one –
it doesn't scratch at all

Sweet inheritance – I'll keep you, I think,
in Memory of Mom.

MISSING HAIKU I

You are in this place
Your legacy resonates
Melodies of love

MISSING HAIKU II

Today I miss you
More than every yesterday
For grief is but love

MISSING HAIKU III

The sound of your voice
The laughter in your soft tone
Still resonates here

MISSING HAIKU IV

Tis joy at the thought
I'll see you when we are raised
Incorruptible

HOME SOON

Names and Memories – they fade
to blend Superior and Sky
and all the vast – between, beyond –
it settles now – Behind

There's nothing left of Manistee
or Saginaw or Frankentrost
or flowers cemented – pink and red –
some flower I know but cannot – Recall

Herman has long since gone to Jesus
and Margaret has laid down her cross
Now their voices – they whisper – unheard but so clear
of moments I've already – Lost

Yet their joy is fragrant – silent but sure
Deeply known, this truth
Their eager delight – the thrill of hope – for
Their baby girl will be – Home soon

INDIANA DEW

Sometimes God's peace settles
Unexpected
Uninvited
Unsolicited
Heavy in the air like
Indiana dew.
Just... heavy –
So heavy it suffocates the firestorm that burns within.
And it settles –
Hanging – hovering – filling up every space
Like a final note in a final chorus resonates throughout a
Cathedral
Seeking minuscule fissures and crannies to fill
While mortals freeze – breath abated – for fear of
disrupting a single vibration.
Because that's what God does.
That's who God is.
He fills up every space.

He cannot be held within the confines
Of the mind
Or the heart
Or even the vast expanse of space in which this life exists.
He is far greater.
He is far more.
He consumes the space
        And everything in it
And lingers awhile –
Holiness consuming unholiness
Loveliness consuming unloveliness
Light consuming darkness
Life consuming death

And it is sacred – this space
      Where the God of Creation lingers
Abiding with all who would stay
Granting peace to the storm
Granting peace to the sea
Granting peace to His children
With His very presence.

TOO SHORT

It is too short –
this life –
sometimes.
And then –
sometimes –
too long.

Too long.
Too hard.
Too sad
my heart.

KRISTI'S ORNAMENTS

I found your sister's ornaments
        in Ziploc and Reebok
        in the bottom right corner of the bookcase
        where they held the weight of a pegless shelf
        and men of great wisdom
And I wondered how many she made in her not-thirty years
And I wondered that she packaged them for sale on
        presumably washed, but still,
        yellow poultry Styrofoam
And I wondered if her fingers ached from the stitching
And I wondered how many more years I should keep them
        their frayed threads and dangling bells
        and worn-through felt that can't even contain their
jolly guts anymore
        (hence the Ziploc)
They aren't hurting anyone in there
And I can't let them go

Even in their worn estate, they weave magical memories –
of stringing popcorn on artificial boughs
        of turkey-shaped cookies with that frosting so
secret we've long-lost your recipe
        of stuffing – oh, the stuffing – the hours of lifting-
not-stirring and slowly adding broth
 between snitches
        of a million lights
                blinking…blinking… blinking…
as my brother seeks the burnt-out bulbs of yesteryear
        of the old, warped vinyl your daddy left behind
Handel never sounded better
        and of the decree sent out by Caesar Augustus

No, not yet
I'll tuck them back where I found them
Where you left them
Ziploc
Reebok
Lewis
Tozer
Mackintosh

LEGACY HAIKU I

My little girl loves
All your teacups that rattle
When the cupboard shakes

LEGACY HAIKU II

Little Lady asks
"Where is Oomah?" And I say –
She's with Jesus now.

We read of Easter
And she shouts, "Here comes Jesus!
Here comes Oomah, too!"

LEGACY HAIKU III

My sister looks like
All the things I love in you
Joy and sorrow – mine

I hear your sharp wit
In the humor of your son
So I laugh and cry

LEGACY HAIKU IV

Your dog misses you
I know because she still waits
Outside your bedroom

CLOSING OF JOHN

I've been searching for Jesus in the Gospel of John
not the One that I've known my whole life
but the One who knows me –
      Right here and right now
      drowning in the remnants
(remnants, trinkets, receipts, garden seeds, bells and sheep and
yarn, yarn, yarn)
of a life well-lived
now laid to rest at the corner of Mallard and Eagle
just in view of the pond where ducks gather to whisper and marvel
at the Fred Astaire Elm where a hundred chickadees swoon
as one about his limbs
      flocking away with glorious swoosh
      then skirts-twirling back into his arms
         (I'm sure she's enjoying the show and
duck gossip)
But I'm left here with the things she couldn't take with her
      not sure where to start or how to let go
of the anguish that comes with recalling –

Like He knew the Samaritan, thirsting for life
And Nathanael, needing to be seen
I long to be known
Right here
      in my kitchen with all the dried-out petals of love
that can't silence sorrow
Right now
      before the first drop of medium-roasted Arabica
touches my lips

Know me, Jesus, I pray.
Find me here.
Don't leave me with the closing of John.

HOPE HAIKU I

You could not take us
We – each – must choose for ourselves
But you showed the way

HOPE HAIKU II

I kept all the leaves
And dried each tender petal
So I'd not forget

The names and faces
Of the lives you touched
In beautiful love

HOPE HAIKU III

Fill this space with joy
Within me and in my home
It comes with daylight

And when morning dawns
And where the evening fades, you
Call forth songs of joy

SEA OF LILACS

What Aaron Heard

In forty years of friendship –
true soul type bond –
and all the struggles we'd known –
I had never felt his heart so raw.
It was palpable.

We met for lunch at the familiar place,
tales of our youth still echoing through the rafters.
And in that sacred space between brothers
I knew he needed to give voice to his sorrow.
As if speaking it
Somehow
would validate his grief.

Heading south on 27, he said.
I drive this road every day –
the weeds, the fields, the rotting barns and broken fences,
the same dotted lines for thirty miles.

And I miss her, he said.

And the silence of the drive
chokes me.
The memories of leaving her over and over
knowing each time could be the last time.
Each hug.
Each word.
Each moment could be the last.
And it's all I could do.
The leaving.

I couldn't stay.
I'd have given anything to stay.
Watching her whither was torture, but I'd have given
anything to stay.
And she knew it.
She understood.
Even as her mind and body failed, she understood.
She always held me tightly and boasted
of the man I had become –
how she loved me and
how she loved her lilacs –
she always thanked me for the lilacs.

She'd wanted a hedge of lilacs on the sandhill side of her
yard
and she'd described it so clearly –
I swear I could see it in her voice.
Best fifty dollars…
Greatest honor of my life…
to buy those first two bushes for her.

I didn't reply.
Not yet.
I understood.
He didn't need answers.
He needed me to hear his confession.
A holy man in best friend's clothing.
That's what he needed.
So I nodded the invitation and my spirit whispered, 'You're
safe here.'

God, I miss her, his eyes drifted far beyond me.
Somewhere beyond the bar.
Beyond the empty tables.

Beyond the kitchen where they prepped the bread and wine.
Beyond earth, he drifted.
I held tight the anchor.

And I couldn't even be there with her as she passed.
It was the worst thing in the world –
lying in that hospital bed after my accident –
Half alive;
Half numb;
Completely broken;
Realizing my gut had been right the last time I left.
It was the last time.

A weak smile darkened his face.
But I got to call from the hospital.
I got to tell her I loved her.
I got to hear her try to say it back.
I think it's the only time we've ever spoken that she didn't mention
the lilacs.

And every day as I drive this road
all of these memories flood me til I'm sobbing down the highway…
Wondering how on earth the accident didn't kill me?
It should have killed me.
That's what I keep hearing.
The doctors.
The nurses.
The guys who ripped my car out from around me.
My family.
Even myself, if I'm honest – I know it's true.
It should have killed me.

Wondering why God sent me back into this sorrow rather
than letting me be there to welcome her Home?
Wondering if she had any idea just how much I adored
her?

Not yet, I thought.
He's almost there.

And that morning –
halfway between here and there
in fields where I've only seen weeds for years –
the sun peeked over the trees, and I saw
a million blossoms in perfect bloom.
Perfect purple.
Perfect row after perfect row.
Mile after mile of lilacs –
As far as I could see, he whispered.
I tried to dismiss the feeling – because she felt so near
and it hurt so much.
But after twenty minutes of nothing but lilacs
I couldn't ignore it anymore.
I pulled over and tried to get out, but I couldn't.
I could barely move.
I opened the window and the fragrance completely
saturated me.
I soaked up every molecule and it undid me.
But I didn't fall apart, you see?
It's like I fell together.
Everything felt right.
For the first time since she passed,
Everything felt right.
And I knew –
She was whole.
She was happy.

She was more alive than ever –
and she wanted me to be whole and happy and alive.
And she sent me a sea of lilacs to prove she'd always be
close to me.

His chin trembled and I knew –
It was time.

"She'll always be close. She's close even now, Brother."

I nodded towards the bar, urging him to turn and look
where the hostess busied herself arranging a fresh bouquet
in a gallon mason jar.

Lilacs.

He looked at me, mouth agape.
And then we laughed.
And then we cried.
And then we toasted Mom.

A Sea of Vignettes

HEIDI'S FOUR SEAMER

It's April.

April in Detroit. And in the living room.

Opening day at Comerica Park.

It's baseball time.

It's knitting time.

Two skeins of sock-weight yarn. One hundred grams apiece. Fifty grams would be fine if it was for one of the girls, but fifty would barely make it past Jeremiah's ankles. Dark blue with a white and orange striping pattern. Looks Tiger-ish. Matching dye lots. The excess already pulled from the center skeins to line up the patterns perfectly. Nobody wants striping socks that don't match.

Two size-two circular needles. Twelve-inch seems to work best.

Needle one. Sixty-four stitches from skein one.

Needle two. Slip thirty-two stitches as if to purl.

Now, holding the needles parallel, slide all the stitches to the far right.

Then, sixty-four stitches from skein two on the second half of needle one.

Back to needle one. Slip thirty-two stitches to needle two.

And don't twist the stitches.

Make sure the skeins don't tangle. Keep them separate.

Now, holding the needles parallel – needle one in front, needle two in back, begin the pattern: Knit two, purl two. Work all the stitches from needle one onto the opposite end of needle one, then turn your needles and work all the stitches from needle two onto the opposite end of needle two.

I know it doesn't make sense. But it works. Trust me.

Look at that. Ninety-eight miles per hour. Can't even see that coming, much less make contact. That's my Tiger! If I could knit like JV's fastball, my bamboo needles would catch on fire. From windup to ump call, I can knit two or purl two – not both. No sparks are flying here.

A three-inch cuff is about thirty rows. Then straight knit for sixty or seventy rows before shaping the gusset and turning the heel. The foot will take some time. It will take some patience. But if I can get through the heel before today's final out, I can work just on the foot during tomorrow's game. Jeremiah will be delighted. Tiger-colored socks knit during Tiger games.

TACO TRUTHS BY MOMMA HEIDI

My friend Marky once said, "No one chops an onion like Heidi." I think he was trying to weasel me out of a fifth taco.

Nonetheless, there's so much more to life and tacos than the onion. Here are a few taco life truths I leave for the next generation.

Serve tacos two soft tortillas at a time: One to hold the taco fillings and the other to line your plate and catch everything that falls out. I call this the Two-Taco Single Serve.

All tacos deserve freshly shredded cheese. If it's worth cheesing, it's worth shredding. What can I say? I'm an over-a-cheeser.

Mix your Iceberg and Romaine lettuces. It gives you both a crunch and a hint of sweetness. And if you tear the leaves by hand rather than chopping them, they'll stay fresh longer.

Get Roma tomatoes, for goodness' sake. Other tomatoes are too juicy. Romas have a great taco-ish texture and a perfect flesh-to-seed ratio. But don't pre-chop more than you need because the worst taco calamity is leftover, chilled tomatoes that have lost their flavor.

Sour cream should be spread evenly across the tortilla rather than dolloped on top.

Serve cheese- and ranch-flavored corn tortilla chips with tacos. I don't know who told the taco shed, but I've been doing this for years.

Use a fork to get a good, finely broken beef. And if you run out of seasoning, just use the magic orange powder. Nobody can tell.

You must serve guac. Nobody likes it. Nobody wants it. I don't make the rules. But if you're making tacos, you have to serve guacamole. I keep an empty coffee can to collect the leftovers so it doesn't stink up the trash.

No matter how many people you expect, you should double up on taco provisions. Someone else will show up. Someone else always shows up.

No one is allowed to snitch black olives during taco prep. Just... No. Except my favorite son. And my grandchildren. Otherwise, nobody. Well, I am, but I don't really count because, you know, Food Prep Rules: Slicer gets to snitch. Otherwise, no one should be snitching black olives.

Go ahead and make the diced tomato, sweet onion, and cheese queso. Some will snack on it beforehand, leaving less room for tacos (and thus more taco leftovers), and some will brilliantly drizzle it over their tacos. Both are delightful.

Invite the college students after church. Let them play the guitars. Let them wrestle the dog. Let them mow the lawn. Let them eat another taco. You can always make more.

Please don't tell Marky, but there really is no secret to chopping the onion. You just do it (you chop; you cry; you savor), and like life, it tastes better when you do it with love.

SNOW ONE LIKE YOU

"Who wants to bring up the first bin?" Mom asked.

The day had settled from traditions into a tryptophan daze. My siblings relaxed in the living room, barely awake. The little ones were limp on the floor with exhaustion or sugar coma from Mom's cookies. I wrote about them all in my head, knowing it would be forgotten before I could find a pen. My sister asked if anyone would drink coffee if she made it. We all would; you can't have pumpkin pie without coffee. But besides the pie, the best part of Thanksgiving was about to begin, and coffee was a must.

Mom was ready for her snowmen. It was time.

My brother cracked a joke about his back (which also cracked) as he pulled himself from the sofa and headed to the basement. He returned, carrying a red 64-quart tote sparkling from unintentional snowman-glitter exposure.

Mom clapped her hands as she let out a simple expression of joy and then thanked my brother for carrying the bin. My sister handed Mom her blue snowman mug with coffee and just enough sweet cream to take the edge off, just how Mom liked it. Mom thanked my sister, warmed her hands on the cup, and then set it down on the windowsill to do what she'd been anticipating all day.

Mom pried the lid off the red bin and set it to the side with a smile brighter than the Christmas tree we had adorned with strands of lights and popcorn earlier in the day. She reached down and pulled out the first bundle. Mom delicately unwrapped the blue tissue paper. My sister took the tissue paper from Mom, flattening it to start a pile, while Mom delighted over the ornament.

"Oh! How cute you are, little one! Your little snowman body is made of ice blocks and look at your ice skates! I love your little pompom hat! Oh, my little Ice-Skating Snowman! There's snow one quite like you! Where would you like to be?" Each of us, save those littles who slept, smiled in response.

"He wants to go on the top branch," my brother offered.

"No, he wants to go on the bottom branch," my other brother offered.

"He could skate across the windowsill," my nephew said.

"How about on the piano?" I suggested.

"I know just the place for you," Mom said, leaning into the tree and choosing a branch in the middle.

Mom lifted another tissue-bundle from the bin and unwrapped it, subconsciously handing the white tissue to my sister, who flattened it and placed it on top of the blue tissue. Mom hugged the decoration to her chest.

"Oh! Hello, my Little Drummer Boy Snowman! You have the cutest little candy cane drumsticks! Pahrum-pumpum-pum, little man!" We all laughed. Mom didn't seem to notice.
"Were you there when Jesus was born? There's snow one quite like you! Where would you like to be this year?"

"He says the top branch," my brother offered.

"He says the bottom branch," my other brother offered.

"He could play his drum, parading across the windowsill," my nephew said.

"How about on the piano?" I suggested.

"I know where you belong," Mom said as she leaned toward the tree and chose a branch opposite the ice-skater.

Mom selected a green tissue-covered ornament, unwrapped it, and handed the paper to my sister, who pressed it flat and placed it on the tissue paper pile. Mom gazed lovingly at the small ornament.

"Hello, dear friend. I've missed you, Snowman Angel! I've missed your sparkling gold halo and gold-tipped angel wings. You just light up the sky like you light up my heart, little one! There's snow one quite like you! Where shall we put you?"

"Top branch," my brother said.

"Bottom branch," my other brother said.

"How about the windowsill," my nephew said, "so all the neighbors can see him."

"The piano," I said.

"Oh!" Mom exclaimed, and reaching for a branch near the top, she said, "You should be here with the Big Angel. You can be one of the hosts of heaven saying, 'Glory to God in the highest'!"

"Yes! Top branch!" My brother threw his fists over his head in pretense victory.

Mom reached for the next tissue-wrapped snowman, removed her long-awaited friend, and handed the paper to my sister, who added it to the pile. Mom's face softened, and she held the snowman up for everyone to see.

"My little Grandson Snowman," she beamed. "Hello, my Grandson Snowman friend! My grandson is growing up, but you're a photo of him as a young boy, held together with white felt, wearing a black felt hat. This is the best snowman anyone ever made for me. There's snow one quite like you."

Mom winked at my nephew. He tried not to smile, but the rosy hue of his cheeks betrayed him.

"Aww." My brother tussled my nephew's hair. My nephew grimaced and pulled his hoodie up and over his head to hide his face.

"Where shall we put you this year, Grandson Snowman?" Mom asked.

"Bottom branch," my other brother said.

"Windowsill," my nephew said from his hoodie. "So he can plan his escape."

My sister let out a belly-laugh – the kind only my nephew can evoke in her.

I laughed in response. "The piano."

"I know where I'll put you," Mom said, and selecting a bough in the center of the tree, she placed her arts-and-crafts Grandson Snowman to face the living room. "Right here, where everyone can see you!"

"Perfect," my nephew rolled his eyes behind his hoodie, but he laughed with the rest of us.

Mom stepped out from behind her snowman bin and kissed the top of my nephew's hooded head. Beyond the laughter, I heard Mom whisper to him.

"There's snow one like you."

Mom returned to her bin and pulled out another snowman. Thanksgiving night was just getting started.

ROOM 614 – LANTERN

Momma Heidi called me her honorary daughter.

Her youngest daughter is my nearest and dearest friend, so Momma Heidi took me as an extension of her family. But Momma Heidi was more than my best friend's mom; She was the Momma of my heart. And she knew it. She reveled in it. She loved me and delighted in me in ways my own mother seemed unable. When I graduated from college, Momma Heidi hugged me tight and cried against my hair, whispering how proud she was of me. When B proposed, I was more excited to tell Momma Heidi than anyone, even my best friend. Momma Heidi squealed with delight and couldn't wait to hear how he'd proposed. When we shopped for my wedding dress, Momma Heidi's eyes lit up when I stepped out from the dressing room in 'the one.'

That I was allowed into her world of snowman collecting was only added joy. No matter how hard times were, I found a way to gift Momma Heidi at least one snowman each Thanksgiving. It mattered to her, and that mattered to me.

B and I had found the perfect gift for her this year. Yes, it was a little more expensive than we'd budgeted for; and yes, we could've nickel and dime shopped and Momma Heidi would've been just as thrilled; but we couldn't resist. We splurged only because it was for Momma Heidi. It was the most perfect gift I've ever chosen for another person: A hanging lantern with a snowman scene carved out of each panel and a five-inch LED candle inside. I knew Momma Heidi would love it. I wrapped it in blue tissue paper and placed it inside a snowman gift bag with Momma Heidi's name.

But Momma Heidi got sick. Quickly. Vehemently. Undiagnosably, it seemed (go ahead and get me started on why medical professionals couldn't figure out what was killing this otherwise healthy, active, vibrant woman). Every time I saw her and every time I spoke with my bestie, Momma Heidi was worse. So our perfect gift sat on our kitchen table, reminding me that the woman I loved more than anything in this life was dying.

When my bestie called, it wasn't the news I'd been expecting. Momma Heidi had been in the hospital for two days already. Her kidneys had failed. She had been asleep for so long. Asleep. Unresponsive. Sedated. One of those, or more. I expected, with great fear, to hear that she had slipped away.

But she awakened. That was the update this day before Christmas Eve. Momma Heidi had awakened. The care aid had come and helped her wash her face, brush her teeth, brush her hair, find her glasses, and sit upright in bed. We heard she managed to eat a supper of mashed potatoes, a small Salisbury steak, and hospital-grade peas.

Her face lit up when we entered. Sorrow caught in my throat like turkey too dry; I swallowed hard to force it down. But relief slipped out in a single drop of molten saline upon my cheek. I swiped at it, but Momma Heidi saw.

"What's this, now?" She reached toward me, and somehow, I maneuvered the tight spaces of room 614 – the table, the chairs, the bags, the machines – and landed in her arms just in time to soak the shoulder of her blue hospital gown with my tears. Momma Heidi held onto me, shushing me like a child and stroking my hair. "There, now. Everything's alright, love. Don't cry, honey. I'm here."

"Yes, you are," I said with the truest smile to ever cross my lips and pulled back as B pressed in. My husband was never so rude.

"We're so happy to see you," he choked out as he hugged her.

I nudged him to quit hogging her and excitedly handed her the gift bag. "We've been saving this for you!" I said.

"Oh!" She giggled like a little girl beyond the reaches of death's shadow and said, "Is it Thanksgiving already?"

"It's almost Christmas," B answered, and I saw confusion flash in her eyes briefly, then settle with resignation. "We're sorry we couldn't be with you for Thanksgiving this year. But we wanted to wait and give you your gift in person."

"You're so thoughtful," Momma Heidi answered him. "Can I open it now?"

We urged her to do just that. Momma Heidi oohed and aahed and fussed over every detail of the gift: the glittery snowman bag, the "to Momma Heidi with love" on the tag, the curled white ribbon tied about the strings of the bag, even the plain blue tissue paper. But when she beheld the lantern, her mouth opened wide as she inhaled, and she froze like a snowman.

"I saw you," Momma Heidi whispered breathlessly. She didn't seem to realize we were still there. She touched one of the snowman carvings gingerly, and the realization flooded over her face. "I was lost in the dark, in a storm, and…God said He was sending someone to help me find my way, and I saw you, shining your light for me to come back."

Momma Heidi looked up at me, her eyes wide. "And then I woke up here."

I opened my mouth but couldn't find a single word.

B put his arm around me and reached for Momma Heidi's hand.

When I finally spoke, all I could manage was, "Merry Christmas, Momma Heidi."

ROOM 614 – DOOR

I felt that nudge in my heart. God's nudge: *Heidi, the blue prayer shawl is for Doris.*

But Doris didn't strike me as the praying type, so we made small talk instead. I asked about her children.

Two, Doris answered. A daughter and a son, but they don't care that I'm laid up in the hospital, dying of fluid overload. My son stopped by for a whole ten minutes earlier. For my signature. He's ready to sell my house before I'm even in the grave.

I asked about her husband.

Hell, I hope, she said. At least someone will be there to welcome me.

I urged her not to say such things. I reminded her that God loved her.

Doubt it, she replied. He's never done a thing for me.

I asked whether her parents had ever told her Jesus loves her?

Between beatings? She asked. Sure. Guess I didn't take their word for it.

I whispered her name and told her how sorry I was.

She told me I was lucky, though. My kids were right there by my hospital bed, holding my hand, praying for me,

95

telling me I would make it home for Christmas. I had flowers. I had visitors. Even the nurses smiled at me.

She was right. The nurses smiled at me and couldn't wait to get away from Doris.

I asked if she had a favorite color, hoping to lighten the mood.

She said she didn't have a favorite anything, but blue always reminded her of the lake, and I smiled – finally, something we had in common.

And God nudged me again: *The prayer shawl is for her. Blue. Like the lake.*

A sojourner's prayer shawl, it was called. The knitting produced loose stitches, meandering into lace, a portrayal of the paths we take in this life, so delicate, so intricate, each footstep. I'd just finished knitting it before this fiasco with my health. I leaned to my daughter and whispered for her to go home, pull it out of the green tote in my bedroom, and bring it back here for Doris.

She objected. I understood why. My kidneys were failing, and my coherence had returned like an unexpected tide. She feared it was the last rush of adrenaline. I feared it, too. Still, I insisted she go home. This was more important. I gave her the "I brought you into this world, I can take you out" glare, hoping it was unaffected by my creatinine level, and spoke her full name so she knew I meant business. She finally agreed. She returned forty-two minutes later with the blue prayer shawl.

Neither Doris nor I were allowed up from our beds, so I had my daughter hand her the shawl. I told Doris I was sorry no one had ever told her, but I was telling her: I loved her, and Jesus loved her. I told her I hoped she'd wrap herself up in the shawl long after I was gone and remember how much Jesus loved her, that He urged me to knit this shawl for her before I even knew her. Blue like the lake. Just because she would like it. My body was weak and uncertain, but my heart was resolute with God's love for this woman, and I wondered whether God hadn't allowed my kidneys to fail just to bring me to the hospital at the right time to meet her.

"Whether I go home with my daughter or home to heaven, Doris, I'll be asking God to show you his love."

And Doris wept.

ROOM 614 - WINDOW

My friend Heidi gave me this lovely shawl.

"I love you, Doris," Heidi said, "And Jesus loves you, too."

Nobody's ever loved me. Nobody's ever cared for me. My parents wished I'd never been born. I wish I'd never been born. But Heidi said she loved me, and something in my heart believed her. Heidi's kidneys were failing. She wasn't sure if she was living or dying, and Heidi sent her own daughter away from her side to go home and to bring this shawl – this one, blue because I told her blue reminds me of Lake Superior – to give it to me. That anyone would give me something just because I might like it – well, I tell you, that's never happened before. No one's ever made anything for me. No one's ever cared for me or given me anything; they've always taken whatever they want – use me and leave me. So I don't know. I don't know why I believed Heidi.

"I love you," Heidi said, "And Jesus loves you, too."

When your kidneys shut down, you don't much want for anything except death anyway – so Heidi wasn't just saying it to get something from me. I think Heidi knew I had nothing to offer her.

But this shawl. Heidi knit it herself. A prayer shawl, Heidi called it. She said she spent several weeks working on it, praying that God would show her who it was for and how she knew when we met that it was for me. The yarn is so soft. The stitches like lace. So delicate. So lovely. Just like Heidi. What could she possibly see in me to deserve such a gift? What could she possibly see in me that deserved to be loved? But that's what Heidi said.

"I love you," Heidi said, "And Jesus loves you, too."

The nurse brought me a small plastic bin to collect my personal belongings before discharge. I folded the shawl carefully, afraid I'd somehow ruin it. Then, when no one was watching, I snatched from the garbage can the two pieces of blue tissue paper that had held a Christmas gift a friend brought to Heidi. I shook the glitter from them.

Oh, don't look at me like that. They were clean. They were untorn.

I spread them flat on my hospital bed, placed Heidi's shawl in the center, and wrapped it to keep it safe. I placed the wrapped shawl in the plastic bin and took it home.

I don't know why it mattered so much. I only know that it mattered.

"I love you," Heidi had said, "And Jesus loves you, too."

Heidi said Jesus loved me, and somehow, I knew it was true.

ROOM 614 - EMMANUEL

Mom's knitting needles clacked against each other, the only sound in the hospital room, save for the random blip of the IV monitor. She hadn't knit since Thanksgiving. Doris was discharged this afternoon, so we opened the privacy curtain for the window view. Mom wanted to see the Christmas Eve stars. She had me place her snowman lantern on the windowsill so everyone in town could see its flicker of hope.

We spent an hour watching the live stream of the Christmas Eve service together on my cell phone. Pastor Chad's message brought tears to Mom's eyes, and she nodded, whispering, "Yes… yes, amen," agreeing with every word he spoke of the infant child born to save mankind. There was nothing so lovely as hearing my Mom's mezzo-soprano as we sang Mom's favorite Christmas hymn, *Away in a Manger*, with our church family. The man in the room next door joined in.

But now, we were silent. Mom seemed lost in thought. I was just content just to be near her, just to know God had brought her back to us for a time, just to see her knitting as she used to – as if the past four weeks had been washed away.

"Sarah, let's take a picture," Mom said, a seemingly random suggestion, but I obliged. I slipped in close to her and used my phone to capture a single selfie of us smiling from room 614 this Christmas Eve.

"Can you send that to other people?" Mom asked.

"Sure," I replied. "Who did you want to send it to?"

"Your brothers and sisters," she smiled. "I'm just missing them."

"They would like that. Is there anything you'd like me to say in the message? Or just send the picture?"

"Yes," Mom set her knitting needles on her lap as she thought. "Room 614. Emmanuel. Even here, God is with us."

PRAYING TO BE USED IN THE CHURCH

Heidi was declining.

Her daughter had called the church office to let us know she'd been placed in hospice care.

"Will you come, pastor?" Sarah asked. Of course I would come.

When Heidi first came to our church, she quietly snuck in and out. I saw her, but it would be several weeks before I could catch her for an introduction. She joined our membership class, even though she'd been raised in the Synod – she knew about *the* Church but wanted to know about *our* church. Even in her elder years, she said, she wanted to be in God's house and know what He was doing. She suffered a health crisis that prevented her from finishing the class, and so she spent years simply worshipping as a non-member. But she did, at that. She loved to be within the walls of the church. She loved to be in the place where God's people gathered. She often told me, "I'd rather be a doorkeeper in the house of the Lord than to dwell in tents of wickedness," and I never believed a person more. It encouraged me, all those services as I led the church in prayer, knowing that Heidi's spirit was in fellowship, longing for nothing more than God's presence. It was an honor to pray with such a soul.

When I arrived at their home, Heidi was awake. They had placed her hospital bed in the living room so she would be near family and visitors. Her gray hair was combed neatly.

She smiled, sat up, and even shook my hand and introduced herself. It pricked my heart, but her daughter had told me Heidi may not recognize me, and this wasn't the first dementia patient I'd visited.

Heidi apologized for all the strangers traipsing through the house. I saw nobody – just Heidi and her daughter. I could read the sorrow plain on her daughter's face. I understood. It wasn't worth correcting Heidi. I reassured Heidi and asked about the pile of yarn in her lap. She was hoping to make prayer shawls, she said. Wouldn't this blue make a beautiful shawl?

It would, I agreed, and then asked if she knew that the church had a prayer shawl ministry. She said she had been wanting to get there for some time, but it was hard because her mom worked all day and she wasn't old enough to drive yet. She would always be welcome, I assured her. That would be so nice, she said, and convenient since the church is right next door. I remembered her daughter telling me that Heidi had grown up in the house on their church's property. Her father had been the music minister. Played the organ, I think.

I commented on the lovely upright piano in the room and asked Heidi whether she played. Her dad was teaching her, but her daughter Sarah, Heidi said, she's the true pianist of the family.

We chatted this way for some time: Heidi slipping somewhere between the boundaries of the present, her long-lost childhood, and people and images only she could see; and me reassuring her and changing the topic. The longer I stayed, the more confused she grew. I offered her the Lord's Supper, and she took it. She struggled on the wafer but eventually swallowed it. I asked if I could pray with her before I left and whether she had any specific prayer requests. Heidi's face scftened, and she said, "Pastor, pray that I would be used in the church. I'd rather be a doorkeeper in the house of the Lord than anything."

I smiled at the familiar words.

In the confusion and fear of the disease, there was Heidi, her spirit still longing for only the pleasure of being in God's house.

And we prayed together one last time.

THE WEDDING PARTY

"It's almost time." Heidi whispered faintly.

"For what?" the nurse asked.

"The party."

"Are you going to a party?" The nurse looked surprised. "What's the occasion?"

"I'm not sure how to say it," Heidi replied slowly, "but I think it might be a wedding."

"I love weddings. Is someone in your family getting married?"

"Not exactly," Heidi struggled to speak, "but I'll have to go soon. They're almost ready."

"Is anyone going with you?" The nurse asked.

"I think so," Heidi answered. She paused, as if she'd fallen asleep. The nurse watched her chest, counting the seconds. When Heidi finally took another breath, she said, "I think my brother David is coming to pick me up. Mom and Dad are already there."

"What about your children? Or your ex-husband? Will you see any of them there, Heidi?"

"Not my children, no. Not yet. They'll come a little later, but I'll have to go soon. I think Earl will be there. I hope so. It would be good to talk with him about everything that happened between us before the kids arrive."

"I don't know, Heidi," the nurse laughed, "I'm not sure I'd want to talk with my ex about the things we went through. I'd rather avoid him."

"No, it's not like that," Heidi smiled. "Earl was sick when we were married. He's better now. I think we'll be able to talk and everything will be forgiven."

"You're a strong woman!"

Heidi's eyes drifted and she was still.

"Heidi, the best part of a wedding is the cake. Will there be cake?"

"I'm not sure," she said. "But I'm not sure it will matter."

"Do you know if they'll have dancing and music?"

Heidi laughed weakly. "The dancing just happens, you can't help it. And of course there will be music. There very sound of his voice is music."

"Who?" The nurse asked. "Your ex-husband?"
"Heavens no," Heidi laughed again, then dozed. The nurse counted the seconds as she watched for the rising and falling of Heidi's chest. The space between was growing longer. The gasp of breath was growing more shallow. Heidi was dying.

"Heidi," the nurse whispered, "What will you wear to the wedding?"

"Oh, it doesn't matter what you wear." Heidi smiled. "When you meet him, you'll understand. The king himself gives clean, white garments to everyone who comes."

EPILOGUE
MY FRIEND HEIDI
A Life Pleasing to God
By Barbara Anthony
Read at Heidi's Memorial Service on November 28, 2023

I first met Heidi in the eighties. Our friendship soon began and I am thankful to know it has no end. We both loved the Lord, our families, and our children. We fellowshipped together through good times and challenging times, praying together, encouraging each other, laughing, and crying together.

Heidi, although very busy, always made time to be with me. She juggled raising a family with church events, studying at Northern Michigan University to obtain a Bachelor of Science in Nursing, working, and several other responsibilities. All of these she accomplished on foot, for she had no car for transportation. She not only did well, but she excelled!

> *Clothe yourselves with compassion, kindness, humility, gentleness, and patience. Bear with each other and forgive one another. And over all these virtues put on love… (Colossians 3:12-14)*

This was Heidi!

Her commitment was first to the Lord and because of it, she served others before herself in true humility. She was never boastful or prideful concerning her many accomplishments, but remained steady, hard-working, gentle, peace-loving, kind, trustworthy, while quietly serving the Lord. She was a patient listener, often encouraging and lifting others up!

She knew her strength could only be found in the Lord. She was not Wonder Woman. She struggled with many weaknesses. In her later years, that was especially true, but those difficult times only served to draw her closer to the Lord, becoming more like Him.
Heidi lived a life that was pleasing to the Lord.

> *For we are God's workmanship, created in Christ Jesus for good works, which God prepared beforehand that we should walk in them. (Ephesians 2:10)*
>
> *Be rich in good deeds, and to be generous and willing to share. In this way they lay up treasure for themselves as a firm foundation for the coming age, so that they may take hold of the life that is truly life. (1 Timothy 6:18-19)*
>
> *I have fought the good fight, I have finished my course, I have kept the faith; Henceforth there is laid up for me a crown of righteousness, which the Lord, the righteous judge, shall give me on that day: and not to me only but unto all them also that love His appearing. (2 Timothy 4:7-8)*

And to Heidi, the Lord says:

Well done, good and faithful servant;
Enter thou into the joy of the Lord!
(Matthew 25:33)

Though there is sadness in our hearts today, we are greatly comforted by knowing that Heidi is with the Lord! She is more alive today than she has ever been and what's more, our future is with her. We patiently wait for that day.

Behold, I tell you a mystery: We shall
not all sleep, but we shall all be
changed – in a moment, in the
twinkling of an eye, at the last trumpet.
For the trumpet will sound, and the
dead will be raised incorruptible, and
we shall be changed. (1 Corinthians
15:51-52)

We've been invited to:

...an inheritance that can never
perish, spoil or fade – kept in heaven
for you. (1 Peter 1:3-4)

Heidi lived a surrendered life to the Lord. Now she dwells in unspeakable joy with perfect love and forgiveness through Jesus Christ, King of kings and Lord of lords, to whom be the glory forever and ever.

Amen.

The End.

Acknowledgements

The best part about writing a book is engaging with people you love. And I do, genuinely, love the people I worked with on this project.

CW: You are the best thing that has ever happened to me. You are the best thing that has ever happened to my writing. Thank you for the countless hours of listening, relistening, and re-relistening as I guinea-pigged you with new versions of worn-out words. Thank you for encouraging me, praying with me, believing in me, and loving me.

My Little Lady: My miracle girl. You distract me from writing in the very best way possible. Please don't stop. You make me a better everything. A bushel and a peck, Little Lady, and a doodle-oodle-oodle-oo.

My Siblings: You are the very caregivers for whom I share this book. Your selflessness and sacrifice as we watched Mom's decline spurred me each day to keep going when my depression and despair almost swallowed my life. I'm so amazed by each one of you. I'm so thankful for each one of you.

Barbara Anthony: My momma's forever sister, and so I have only to talk with you when I'm missing her and I am reminded that she's not so very far away. Thank you for speaking what we are unable to say. Thank you for loving us. Thank you for always pointing me back to the hope we have in Christ.

J&B: For all the moments… for all the tears… for the Snowman Lantern… for making sure my family and I ate food… for helping us pay medical bills we couldn't keep up with… and mostly, for loving Momma so well… well… you know.

Jeremiah & Aaron: For the Lilac story. Thank you for allowing me into your friendship to see the deep spiritual connection you share. I hope I've done the story and your friendship justice.

Andy Rogers: Dear Coach. Here it is: My first postcard from the moon. Thank you for helping me find my voice, my courage, and my footing. Next stop, Ceres!

Karen Brough, Robyn Smith, and Evelyn Sherwood: My lifelong friends of one year. *Insert intense sobbing here.* How I thank the Lord for you, my Writing Sisters. Your encouragement and feedback inspire me. Thank you for spurring me on in this journey.

Stephen Smith: With a "ph." There is nothing I love more than picking up the mail and seeing your handwriting with my name spelled correctly. Your wit and wisdom still astound me after a quarter of a century. You're still doing the work of a teacher, inspiring me to be better, challenging me to dig deeper, and refusing to accept mediocre when I can at least bring "a little bit better than mediocre." Thank you for sharing your words with me. Thank you for sharing your friendship with me. Thank you for using blue ink rather than red. Love, Sarah with an "h."

Eileen Smit: Many of these words were penned during the respite you provided to me. They were some of the only moments of processing I had during Mom's decline. I cannot thank you enough for those moments. I cannot thank you enough for your continued friendship and the hugs we share on random neighborhood rendezvous. Belle and I are watching for you on our walks.

Coralie Voce: For singing with me. For singing with Mom. For the many hugs. For the many reminders that I was not to blame. For the gentle presence you offered as we neared the sacred moment of Mom's passing. And for putting your eyes on this manuscript as I struggled to move forward in my grieving process.

Reverend Chad Ott, Reverend Daniel Ondov, and the ministry staff at Redeemer Lutheran Church: Thank you for loving and serving my mother and so many others as they near the end of their earthly lives. Thank you for loving CW, Little Lady, and me as we walked this path. We don't have big enough words to express our hearts.

www.ingramcontent.com/pod-product-compliance
Lightning Source LLC
Chambersburg PA
CBHW070341130626
46556CB00007B/2975